f r i e n d l y   p h o

MW01689194

Jungle Journey

By Cindy Leaney

Illustrated by Sue King and Peter Wilks

ROURKE CLASSROOM RESOURCES

The path to student success

Note to Parents and Teachers/Educators

Before reading: Ask your child what this book might be about. Read the title aloud together. What sound does the letter *j* make in *jungle*? Remind your child to listen for that sound in the story.

Written by Cindy Leaney
Designed by Ruth Shane
Illustrated by Sue King & Peter Wilks
Project managed by Gemma Cooper

Created and Designed by SGA and Media Management
18 High Street, Hadleigh, Suffolk, IP7 5AP, U.K.

P. O. Box 3328, Vero Beach
Florida, 32964, U.S.A.
Editor: Patty Whitehouse

Printed in China

ISBN 1-58952-910-3

Jungle Journey

I'll jump out of my pajamas and
jump into my jeans.

Today's our jungle journey. Now where is my canteen?

This is a major project. We need to think things through.

We need to take these jars and
that jump rope, too.

Do we really need the jars?
And what's the jump rope for?

We're going to the jungle to find
things, to explore!

We're going to look for jewels, who knows what we will see?

We might see wild animals–like a jaguar in a tree.

For a journey to the jungle we need a jeep or a jet.

You're joking. We're just kids.
We can't drive or fly yet.

We'll just have to walk, or maybe we could jog.

If we get really tired, we can
jump on the dog.

I'm a little jumpy, to tell you the truth.

I just saw a jaguar jump onto that roof!

That wasn't a jaguar, that was just a cat.

You have got the jitters.
It's as simple as that.

I just saw a jackal with jumbo jaws!

That wasn't a jackal.
That was a dog you saw.

No jumping jaguars, no jewels,
no jeep, or jet.

But even so, our jungle journey was the very best trip yet!

Game time!

Match the words from the story to the pictures.

1. jaguar
2. jackal
3. jump rope
4. jeep
5. jet
6. jewels

Answers: **1.** e, **2.** d, **3.** f, **4.** a, **5.** b, **6.** c.